Rewire Your Brain

How to Declutter Your Mind, Make New Habits, End Anxiety and Create New Positive Outcomes For Yourself.

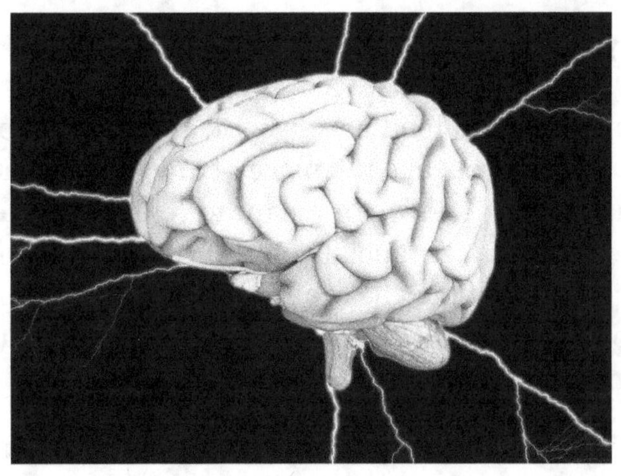

Noah Grayton

"Rewire Your Brain"

Legal & Disclaimer

advisor) before using any of the suggested remedies, techniques, or information in this book.

Upon using the contents and information contained in this book, you agree to hold harmless the Author from and against any damages, costs, and expenses, including any legal fees potentially resulting from the application of any of the information provided by this book. This disclaimer applies to any loss, damages or injury caused by the use and application, whether directly or indirectly, of any advice or information presented, whether for breach of contract, tort, negligence, personal injury, criminal intent, or under any other cause of action.

You agree to accept all risks of using the information presented inside this book.

You agree that by continuing to read this book, where appropriate and/or necessary, you shall consult a professional (including but not limited to your doctor, attorney, or financial advisor or such other advisor as needed) before using any of the suggested remedies, techniques, or information in this book.

Table of Contents

Introduction

What does the brain control?

The brain is a delicate instrument. It's a follower of the mind, and thus it does what the mind directs it to do. Whether the command is deliberate or expressed automatically, it has to adhere to the instructions. When the body is under control of positive thoughts, it works in your favor. We can say people who have **good emotional health and are acutely aware of their thoughts**, behavior, and feelings, are the ones who have learned ways to cope with stress, anxiety and daily problems which are part and part of life.

However, if you poison your body with **negative thoughts**, the body will rapidly deteriorate and eventually be engulfed with diseases and worry. Negative thoughts are rooted and originate from the mind, YOUR mind, and they are conveyed clearly when the body is sick.

Negative thoughts have been known to cause real harm to the body, and in fact, they can kill a man with surprising speed. Individuals who are prone to suffer from negative thoughts are those who live in fear and doubt.

Anxiety plays a major part in demoralizing the body as it leaves the body and mind wide open to diseases. If you continue to propagate foul thoughts, your body will continue to have immoral and poisoned blood. A clean mind and heart will give birth to a clean body. Every action is based on thought because thought is the source of action and life.

<u>Even if you switch to a healthy diet, without changing your thoughts, it is equivalent to covering up the root of the problem</u>. But once your thoughts are pure, the change of diet will be just an additional ingredient. Good habits emanate from good thoughts. The same is true of the flip side. Therefore, guarding the mind is as important as perfecting your body. It is unfortunate that the majority are overwhelmed with envy, disappointment, maliciousness, and despondent thoughts that burglarize the health and grace of the body.

It is possible to improve on emotions only if you understand your feelings and how to control them. Also, you need to know the cause of your anxiety, sadness, and stress, and then you will be able to maintain your emotional health. Living a balanced life is one way you can control your emotions. Today's life is moving at the speed of a bullet, and many activities like school and problems at work can lead to negative feelings. You may pretend to be happy, yet you are stressed, upset, or anxious. Although it is advisable to deal with these negative feelings, focusing on positive things in your life is what you need to do. You also have to let go of some things in your life, those that make you feel overwhelmed and stressed.

Calm your mind and body using methods like meditation to bring emotions back to balance. Also, we earlier saw that people who live in fear are the ones who are affected most by negative thoughts. Thus, developing resilience is imperative. People who are resilient have a better chance of coping with stress in a healthy way. Then again, you must know how you can express your feelings, because good changes can be as stressing as bad habits.

Chapter 1: The Battle of the Brains

In the 1960s, psychologist and Nobel Prize winner Roger W. Sperry made a groundbreaking discovery. His research showed that the brain, rather than being one unified mass; was actually divided into two hemispheres, each one having different and contrasting functions. So different are the functions that it appears as if we have two separate brains, hence, the two hemispheres are more commonly called the "right brain" and the "left brain". The following table displays a few of these functions.

Right Brain Functions	**Left Brain functions**
Creature thinking	Linear thinking
Visualization	Sequencing and spatial recognition
Intuition and imagination	Logic and mathematical thinking
Emotional, spontaneous thinking	Analytical, fact-oriented thinking
Holistic thinking, such as putting	Thinking in words

words into context

Strengths: Arts, Music

Strengths: Mathematics, mechanics.

Controls muscles on the right side of the body

Controls muscles on the left side of the body

<u>**Is there a conflict?**</u>

People with more dominant left-brain characteristics tend to have the personality traits associated with the left hemisphere; they are linear and analytical in their thinking, tend to be good at mathematics and mechanics and respond to life situations in a logical and calculated manner. People with right brain characteristics tend to be creative, imaginative and spontaneous. They respond to life situations more emotionally and intuitively. They are artistic, musically inclined and creative.

Despite this apparent contrast, the left and right brains don't work individually, nor are they in conflict with each other. The more dominant side does not cancel out the less dominant side. People with predominantly right brain qualities can be data scientists while with people with left-brain powers can be more artistically gifted. Nor should we label people as "right-brained" or "left-brained".

Science has shown this to be a false assumption. A 2013 study on over 1000 participants whose brains were scanned with MRI imaging concluded that there was no dominant side. The participants used both the left and right brains interchangeably depending on what they were doing. A more dominant left or right brain simply means that we lean more towards <u>certain ways of thinking</u> and behavior based on our character and personality.

We develop personality traits that may be predominantly left brain or right brain, but we do not have one brain that is dominant over the other.

The left and right hemispheres are interconnected by a series of neurological pathway and are constantly communicating with each other, exchanging signals and information. This interconnection is vital for us to be able to function as normal human beings. We don't use only one side of the brain when performing a function. For example, when we are in a conversion, the left brain processes information and allows us to understand the words being spoken while the right brain helps us understand their context and meaning. Having a conversation with another person, therefore, would be impossible without the two hemispheres working together.

Rewiring the emotional right brain

Our concern, however, is with "rewiring" the right brain where emotions are found, as emotions play a more important role in shaping our behavior. The good news is that our brain has the ability to reorganize itself and constantly adapt to new thought patterns and therefore, it is ideal for learning. This makes it possible for any person to create a tailor-made plan to rewire emotional patterns that are negatively influencing their perception and behavior.

A good example of this is irrational anger. Some people react to certain situations with disproportionate anger, such as coffee being served cold at a restaurant, mediocre customer service at a store, or even a colleague making a well-meant criticism. Many people have anger issues because a certain past experience triggers their mind to respond in this way. By continuing to respond with anger to subsequent experiences, the mind has learned to make it a habit. To put it another way, this person's mind has learned to over-personalize, meaning to take even the most mundane situations personally. Think of "Road Rage" as a prime example of this.   This is the sort of issue where the mind needs to be rewired to **respond** differently.

Emotions are vital to our lives. If we relied only on our left brain functions, we would be no more than robots, mechanically going through the motions of living. It is our emotions, both positive and negative, that give us our individuality and make us human. Among the wide range of emotions we experience are positive emotions like love, happiness, gratitude and fulfillment. Negative emotions such as fear, worry, anger and envy can destroy our well-being and if left unchecked, lead to some very self-destructive habits – and in some cases, even addictions.

Negative emotions such as anxiety and fear can be beneficial up to a point, as they may help us avoid danger and harm or push motivate us to compete and excel, but we should never allow them to be the controlling emotions in our lives.

Take a moment now to take stock of where you stand. What emotions do you feel are negatively affecting your relationships and career? Are you hesitant to take a relationship further out of fear of rejection? Are you always worrying about the future? Are you missing opportunities because you overthink things to death before deciding to make a move? Are you harming family relationships through irrational anger? Are you stick in your career, because you worry that you're not qualified enough to get a better job?

These are the types of emotions you need to delete from your mind because they are holding you back from achieving happiness and success.

Who's the culprit?

Now that we have learned a little bit on how your mind works and the fact that the left and right brains complement and support each other, rather than being at odds; where does the problem lie? The problem lies with us; our brain is merely doing what we have programmed it to do. Read on to find out why and what we can do about it.

Chapter 2: We Are Our Own Worst Enemy

Stress is the curse of our modern world. Despite all the cutting-edge inventions developed for our ease and comfort, the gadgets and appliances that make our lives so much easier, and despite the amazing digital revolution, we have nowhere near the content and peace of mind that our grandparents and great parents had. We are constantly striving to compete, to be better parents, better wives and husbands, higher achievers, more successful in our careers, and earn enough money to meet ever-rising expenses. Anxiety, worry and fear of the future are the modern-age diseases.

They are the major obstacles to happiness and peace of mind, and in fact, may sometimes be so crippling that they bring our lives to a total standstill. Not to mention how constant worry, stress and overthinking can affect us physically, dragging us into a vicious cycle that is becomes harder and harder to break out of.

It is crucial to understand the following fact: It's not life circumstances that prevent us from achieving what we want, nor is it the way our brains are made. It's how we have trained our minds to think and react.

Everything originates with your thoughts about the present situation. How do you view your situation? Is it possible to

view it a different way so that you can get a different result?
Yes, and we are our almost always our own biggest enemy.

Cognitive Fusion

Cognitive fusion is the linking of thoughts to experiences. Say you are in an elevator that stalls midway down or up. You're stuck inside for a few minutes and understandably, you start to panic. But the problem is quickly fixed and the elevator continues on its way and you reach your destination safe and sound. It's a scary experience, yes; but the odds of it happening again are very slim indeed. However, the next time you enter an elevator, you remember the experience; your brain remembers how you reacted and once again, you will feel panic. Unless you intervene and TRAIN your mind to react differently, this will happen each time you get into an elevator and over time, it will become a phobia. This is called cognitive fusion. The experience becomes "fused" to a particular reaction to your brain. In other words, your mind forms a habit.

Now, you have two choices here; Either you avoid elevators altogether (not an appealing option when you have an important job interview on the 15th floor), or, retrain your mind to react differently. You can use cognitive fusion to work for you instead of against you.

Cognitive fusion occurs when the mind starts to interpret thoughts as facts. In this example, it believes that when you step into an elevator, it will stall. And because you reacted with fear and panic the first time this happened, your brain believes you are in danger. It will warn you of this danger by retriggering those feelings of fear, anxiety and panic. You see, your brain is actually trying to help you based on the information YOU gave it the first time this happened!

In cognitive fusion, The mind "fuses" the thought to the experience and reacts in the same way each time that experience is repeated. It does this with both positive and negative experiences. For example, let's say you are at a beach and witness an amazing sunset over the ocean. You experience feelings of wonder, joy and tranquility as you watch the beautiful colors spread across the horizon and slowly fade. Your brain perceives the sunset is a positive experience that makes you feel good and will trigger those same feelings each time you see a sunset until they become fused to the experience.

Can you see how we might unknowingly train our minds to harm and hinder rather than help? The other side of the coin is that we can also train our brain to help rather than hinder. Realizing that we can rewire our mind to react the way we want it to is a life-changing concept. Let's continue a bit more with our exploration of the brain.

The Cortex and the Amygdala, Two Anxiety pathways

Why do we experience anxiety and worry?

The human brain has the unique ability to imagine the future. No other living creature can do this (which is, perhaps, a blessing in disguise!). However, many of us tend to envision adverse rather than positive outcomes, especially when we are under stress. As a result, we become anxious or worried. Again, we train our brain to perceive the future as something bad or harmful and this triggers negative thoughts and emotions.

Anxiety is created in the brain through two "anxiety pathways", the cerebral cortex and the Amygdala. They are located in different areas of the brain but their function is similar.

The Amygdala

This is an almond-shaped cluster of neurons found deep inside the temporal lobe. It is responsible for processing thoughts and emotions that have to do with survival, such as fear, anger, pleasure and anxiety. It also determines where memories are stored on the brain based on the strength and type of emotions involved on the experience that creates the memory.

The amygdala cannot differentiate between actual events and thoughts, and responds to both in the same way. For example, if you are in real danger it will trigger a "fear and flight" response to help you avoid or confront the danger. . Likewise, if you 'think' a certain situation is dangerous when there is no real danger, the amygdala will trigger the very same fear and flight response.

The Cerebral Cortex

The cerebral cortex is a very thin layer ranging between 1.5 mm. to 5 mm. that covers the cerebrum. It is commonly referred to as "gray matter" because the nerves are not insulated making it appear gray, unlike the other parts pf the brain which appear white. It is responsible for several functions, including determining personality and intelligence, planning an organization, language processing and sensory functions and motor functions. The cortex also helps us to experience and interact with our world.

An example of cortex-based anxiety is when in certain situations, our mind jumps ahead and envisions a negative outcome. For example, you receive a phone call from someone who hasn't contacted you in a long time. You immediately imagine that the caller has bad news, perhaps a death in the family, and you start to feel worried and anxious. Instead, the person is calling to invite you to a wedding. This is how the cortex works to trigger anxiety.

Controlling the Cortex and the Amygdala

You can control the negative emotions triggered by the cortex and amygdala simply by controlling your thoughts. Always remember that your mind is not the culprit; it is simply responding to the <u>thoughts you feed it</u>. Psychologists who specialize in this field advise us to stand up to our thoughts, and to challenge them. Is that elevator really going to stall every time you step into it? Is it really likely to happen again, probably not. Therefore, the fear and panic are unfounded. Pessimists especially need to do this and realize that their thoughts do not and cannot control the future. Exchanging negative thoughts for positive ones will not control the future either, but having an optimistic perception will create a better future experience for you.

Cognitive Restructuring

The first step in the process of rewiring your mind is to step back and observe a certain thought. Do not try to push it away but don't yield to it or believe it either. Simply acknowledge the thought. Next, question the thought and finally, challenge it. What evidence do you have that this is going to happen? How likely is it to happen? Are you absolutely sure that this will be the outcome? Is it realistic to suppose that this will be the outcome?

Cognitive restructuring is the process of learning to be suspicious of negative thoughts and to generate opposing thoughts.

Start with your most recurring anxiety and fear-inducing thoughts. Observe, acknowledge, and challenge them. Then, **replace** them with thoughts that are more realistic. Doing this repeatedly will literally start the process of transformation - the wiring of your mind will begin to change, physically.

Thought exchange repeated is proven to work, and actually forms new synaptic connections.

Fear thought example: "I can't do public speaking because everyone will think I am an idiot and laugh at me."

Exchange for: "It is possible I can become good at public speaking by practicing and attending toastmaster events. I don't know what the audience is REALLY thinking, maybe they envy me?"

Let's illustrate this with another example. Whenever you receive a utility bill, you start to feel anxious and worried. You're on a tight budget and are afraid it will be too high. What if you can't pay it? What if you can't pay the next one? The bills will keep piling up until your electricity is cut off. You work yourself up into a frenzy of worry, all before opening the bull!

Instead, begin the process of positive restructuring by doing the following: Step back from your first thought, that the bill will be too high. Observe and acknowledge the thought... it makes you feel worried and anxious. Now, challenge the thought. Is it reasonable to get so worked up about a utility bill? How do I know it's going to be much higher than what I normally pay? Haven't I always managed to pay my bills before? If worse comes to worst, I can borrow the money, or take it out of my savings, can't I? What's the big deal? When you repeat this process over and over again, there will come a time when that utility bill will arrive and your mind will think, "Oh, it's the utility bill. Okay..." You're not exactly leaping with joy but you're not anxious or worried, either. You can do this with every recurring negative thought that you have.

Now, let's learn how we can generate positive thought and train our brain to turn them into habits.

Chapter 3: Brain Training – Is It Real and Does It Work?

Does brain training actually work? That depends on your definition of effectiveness. In the past, brain training has claimed to increase an IQ score. Additionally, brain training games will often make an overarching or umbrella promise to make you "smarter." What does that even mean, make you smarter?

The outright answer is that brain training can teach you to:

- Adopt different mindsets

- Become more adaptive to situations and environments

- Increase reasoning and rationalization skills

- Understand complexities in content and context

Will brain training teach you to be smarter? No. However, it will enable you to use your knowledge and skillset better. Brain training is not learning, it's exercise. You're stretching, flexing and building strength in a muscle. Unfortunately, there is no method of heavyweight lifting for your brain. Instead, think of brain training like yoga or golf. You're working out muscles and getting good exercise, but you won't see outstanding results on your health overnight. Starting brain training is something that you might want to ease into over the course of a few weeks. Building up your brain training exercises can help ensure that you keep your exercise sessions consistent with the exercised involved varied.

When setting clear and realistic expectations for brain training, you can evaluate this process with an inversion lens. Ask yourself how many times you think you had to pick up a fork before it became natural. A hundred times maybe, but possibly closer to a hundred thousand.

From the time you were born, you began developing skills that you still use today. Some of these skills you probably use multiple times within an hour such as lifting a cup without spilling. Brain training will rely on the same notion however, it's much more fun.

When brain training works, it carefully balances repetition with variance. Perhaps you remember in grade school, spelling the same four or five-letter words repeatedly. Now spelling "that" or "have" is a subconscious act. You probably cannot say the same for spelling words that did not fall into those practice sessions such as "nausea" or "separate." Don't worry, brain training is not spelling practice, many brain training games or activities are fun, interactive and approach knowledge in a general sense.

The basis of brain training is not to make each specific act natural. Instead, it strives to create the feeling of muscle memory and apply it across the board to any number of situations. Popular apps tend to focus on memory games, attention division, and spatial management as they can apply to many areas of daily life. Focusing on your ability to move from one task to another quickly may help you go from working in Microsoft Word to Excel. Or answering emails to inputting data. It could even help you change gears from playing with your kids to making your shopping list. The general nature of the brain training activities helps to build that feeling of familiarity in switching from one task to another quickly. Although you won't likely bet matching Tetris squares in real life, the activity develops more skills than what you see at first blush.

Yes, brain training is effective, and you can explore many other opportunities both at home, on your phone, and in your community. We've established that it's not about boosting your IQ but can impact your efficiency and effectiveness in everyday tasks. You probably have a good grasp on how this happens as well through repetition and the manipulation of memory, familiarity and building new mental bridges.

The first known commercial endeavor to market brain training was CogniFit in 1999. As interest grew among the public brain game books were released, and more companies emerged.

However, brain training was present long before 1999. Mnemonic systems and Pelmanism have been around for more than 100 years. In some cases, these were packaged into sessions or booklets that you can study. In other cases, they were methods used in a classroom.

All the same, Pelmanism is the foundation of much of the brain training in progress today. It relies on creativity, concentration and attention. On a rather important note, these three factors are the key facets to many card, chip, and pencil and paper games that came before Pelmanism.

In addition to finding brain training in games that families would play around the table, you may be familiar with popular brain training publications. Popular Mechanics started with the intent of widely distributing Pelmanism programs on concentration or memory. While Popular Mechanics has long since adapted their content, it's clear that brain training has been a common interest among people over the last few centuries.

Until recently, methods of brain training have focused primarily on individual exercise. Crossword puzzles and more were simply printed for those interested to use as they pleased. However, that has changed drastically with apps and entire companies dedicated to developing brain training programs.

Do you need a coach?

Historically, brain training shows that you don't need anything than practice material and a desire to develop. You can pay for the premium options of brain training apps or sign up with the still available CogniFit programs. Finding a coach isn't necessary by any means, although it can impact your training.

As with any other exercise, a coach can ensure that you stay on track and assess if you're reaching your goals. They can help you set realistic milestones and change your routine if they notice a lack of progress. For many people, that's a huge benefit and for others, it's unnecessary.

Hiring a coach for brain training may be reasonable for someone who is experiencing troubles with memory, attention, and number handling. These issues may be attributed to recent accidents or injuries. Retraining your brain is a common step in recovery after a traumatic accident. Rehabilitation programs will often work with patients throughout this step using flashcards or memory exercises. That doesn't mean you have to stop there. After your mandatory rehab session, you can use apps to work alone or find a coach that understands your mental and physical needs.

If you are looking for brain training as a way to recover from a traumatic event, ensure that the training will not affect your medical recovery. Overworking yourself or pushing yourself too hard can lead to undue stress. Stress is one of the many factors that can delay your full recovery. If you're worried about returning to work or establishing a routine similar to what you had prior to the injury, be careful to pace yourself. Again, it's worth noting that even constant brain training with a well-established coach will not have an overnight effect. Instead, take brain training on with the mentality of a low-impact sport. To get good at it, you need to do a little bit every day for a long time.

So, what should you expect from brain training?

Unfortunately, because any brain training program can fluctuate so drastically from another, it's hard to say that you will see any set of tangible results quickly. It all depends on what activities and games you implement into your day. Overall, you'll want to create a full program for yourself so that you have clear goals to reach and a structure to guide you towards them. As you read through the tips, tricks, and many activities here take note of what catches your eye and tailor your brain training program to encompass what you're hoping to achieve.

If you're trying to improve your memory, then focus on activities that will engage your working memory and reshape your implicit memory reaction to events. Alternatively, if you need to improve your concentration, you might need to spend time holding a glass of water at arm's length (yes this works).

How can you decide what you need to work on?

You likely already have some goals, but if they're general such as, "become more intelligent" you'll need to dive into what that means to you. When it comes to outright intelligence, you might want to improve your speaking skills, become more articulate, calculate sums in your head quickly, increase vocabulary, increase knowledge or make faster intelligent decisions. These are aspects that people often associate with intelligence and are all things you can work on through brain training.

If these look like your goals, you might want to try playing cribbage, learning a new language, learning a new word each day, and read more often. There are numerous activities you can do to improve these skills, and many are fun. As part of your brain training, you'll see that there are clearly activities that will help you and others that won't contribute much of anything to your goals. Keep this in mind as you read.

Now, you might want to build your ability to communicate or understand people more clearly. Reading will likely be your go-to brain training event in this case, along with other language-based games or activities. From crossword puzzles to book circles, developing your language skills can be fun. But these skills take a long time to improve as you've spent years, or probably decades, building up your current language habits. You'll notice as part of brain training that you are fighting against your current habits and trying to forge new habits at the same time. Not only is this true on an observable level, but it's apparent on a brain science level as well. During brain training, many activities will help create new pathways in your brain, or in essence, rewiring.

The variances of brain training from one person to another are among the many reasons why it has come under so much scrutiny. But it's also a reason to avoid brain training programs hosted through third-parties. You can, and should, create your own brain training program. With the internet and a massive library available on brain training, you can decide what will provide the biggest impact for you. Preset or template brain training programs may only teach you the skills necessary to accomplish those tasks.

For example, a game within a popular app, Lumosity, claims to help you switch from one way of thinking to another quickly. The game, called Ebb and Flow, requires you to swipe across the screen either in the direction that leaves are drifting or the direction that they are floating. This game, in particular, came under fire for providing false claims or tangible results. When placed in other scenarios, many players were not capable of adapting the skill learned in Ebb and Flow. That means that they basically only learned how to play this game and have a skill that is not applicable anywhere else.

Because of issues such as this where people cannot adapt the training, it can make some brain training seem like a lost cause. That's not the case, but it does place a great deal of importance in finding the correct format and the right games for you. If you want to learn to switch between different tasks quickly, then you need a game or activity that enacts that skill in a variety of different formats. To achieve this, you may utilize two or more different games so that you can rotate between them. For example, playing Ebb and Flow one day, then playing a game variant of the Stroop test to manipulate your ability to focus on changing information. Even with games such as Ebb and Flow that don't translate well into physical results, you can manipulate the way you train your brain to extract those skills and implement them in different ways.

Brain training can become a great source of power for you. Everything that you can take away from brain training is in your control, and many people like that, but many others find that level of control intimidating. Ultimately you will know what is or what is not working for you. Using tips and tricks to make some more challenging tasks easier or more enjoyable can help you receive bigger payoffs from tasks that might have seemed like a drag.

While you read through, focus on having fun. You're not in school, and no one is forcing you to take on these tasks, so enjoy them. When you start brain training, always start with a game. As you'll read about soon, games are not only fun but offer many benefits for your brain. Without a doubt, you can find a game that delivers some of the results you're hoping to see from your brain training program.

Chapter 4: How the Brain Forms Memories

Learning and forming memories are complex processes, there are 100 billion neurons in your brain that are constantly at work communicating with thousands of other neurons at any given time. Neurotransmitters that travel through the synaptic gaps bind to specific receptor molecules located in the neighboring neuron. *Eventually, recurring experiences (stimuli) create synaptic connections and form a neuronal circuit or connections (pathway) which is actually memory formation.* When the same stimulus happens again, you react almost instinctively from memory recall. This is the rationale behind the 10,000-hour principle, which states that 10,000 hours of deliberate practice is needed to master any type of skill.

The brain activities involved in memory are complicated and may be simplified as follows:

- Creating a memory

Our brain sends signals in a particular pattern depending on the event we are experiencing. Consequently, connections between the neurons, called synapses, are created.

- Consolidating the memory

Memories that are deemed insignificant are inevitably discarded. Those that need to be committed to long-term memory are consolidated for easy retrieval when needed later on. This process of sorting out memories happens during sleep, when the brain recreates the events of the day.

- Declarative memories **are enhanced during slow-wave sleep. Declarative memories include factual information, previous experiences and concepts that were intentionally collected for sorting and storage.**

- Non-declarative memories, **on the other hand, are enhanced during rapid eye movement (REM) sleep. Non-declarative memories include procedural memories, which help you perform certain tasks without conscious awareness of these previous experiences.**

Recalling the memory

Memory recall refers to the subsequent re-accessing of information and events from past experiences, previously processed and stored in the brain. Simply put, it is what is called remembering. During recall, a pattern of neural connection gets activated in response to a similar event. The brain only echoes its perception of the event as if it is happening in real time.

These replays, though, are not strictly identical to the original. The real experience will always be different from the memory recalled because it is already mixed with new information and old memories, thus remembering could be thought of as a creative re-imagination of the recurring event.

Memories are not organized in our brains like books in a library. It's more like jigsaw puzzle pieces stored in separate parts of the brain linked together by neural networks or circuitries. Remembering therefore involves revisiting the pathways formed during the previous experience. The strength of these pathways will determine how quickly memory retrieval will occur. Recall reloads a long-term memory from storage into short-term or working memory, where it can be accessed and used. It then re-stores the new memory from the experience into long-term memory for re-consolidation and strengthening.

Chapter 5: Addiction

When we think of addictions, most of us associate the term with drugs or alcohol but the definition spans much, much more. You may discover after reading this chapter that you have an addiction but never realized it! **Addictions are habits that are much harder to break because your mind associates them with pleasurable and positive outcomes.**

Unlike a regular habit, an addiction is characterized as being an uncontrollable craving or compulsion that when satisfied, gives us immense feeling of pleasure.

The difference between an addiction and a habit is that we can control or break a regular habit much more easily than we can an addiction. If left unchecked, addictions can have disastrous effects on our lives and on those around us. The great news is that many addictions can be cured with neuroplasticity but require super strong commitment and unfailing practice. All addictions have their basis in emotional issues.

Types of addictions

Substance dependencies

This type of addiction is commonly known as "substance abuse."

It includes alcohol and drugs like; cocaine, heroin, crack, opium, etc. Prescription drugs and painkillers also fall into this category as well as smoking.

Behavioral dependencies

These are called "Compulsion disorders" and include gambling, pornography, addiction to sex, compulsive lying, self-harm such as cutting oneself and eating disorders like Anorexia and Bulimia.

Addictions you might not have known were addictions

These behaviors may appear benign at first glance but if they get out of control can be very damaging. These include technology addictions to gaming and social media, kleptomania, shopping and working (hence the terms "shopaholic" and workaholic"), compulsive spending, pyromania (a compulsive desire to start fires) and even exercising/working out.

"Socially acceptable" addictions

These types of addictions are considered normal and culturally acceptable, which, one might argue makes them more dangerous!

As an example, coffee shops and internet cafes are some of the most popular places these days, yet they may be inadvertently feeding caffeine and technology addictions. Of course, not everyone is addicted to caffeine but the number is high enough. Yet, society accepts coffee drinking as normal and even trendy, as proven by the "custom-coffee" bars that are popping up everywhere.

The same goes for smoking. True, it's getting harder to smoke in many places nowadays but nonetheless, it is still a socially accepted addiction as long as you don't bother others with your secondhand smoke.

The same applies to cola and energy drinks. We don't tend to think of all of these as addictions until we miss our cup of morning coffee or after-breakfast cigarette and start to feel irritable or get a headache - classic withdrawal symptoms.

Or, how many times have you heard somebody jokingly say, "I'm a total zombie until I've has my cup of morning coffee". That's because they're addicted to caffeine.

Working too much, shopping sprees and exercise are also socially accepted behaviors that could become addictions.

Symptoms of addiction

Regardless of the type of addiction, the symptoms are similar:

- An uncontrollable desire to consume the substance or engage in the behavior

- Total lack of control to stop or curb the behavior

- Continuing the addictive behavior despite the negative consequences a person know it has.

- Withdrawal symptoms that can range from nausea, headache, itching and stomach cramps, to irritability, anger, rage or even violence.

How addiction is created in the brain

Addiction starts as a type of "self-medication" to alleviate physical pain or to numb emotional pain, such as loneliness, emptiness, grief or lack of self-worth.

When the substance or behavior alleviates pain or relaxes you and gives you pleasure, your brain registers this, thinking it is good for you.

Repetition of the action and the pleasure it gives further confirms to the brain that this is something you find relevant and "positive" and so, the neural pathway is created.

The difference between an addiction and a habit that you know is negative, such as worry or anxiety, is that an addiction **makes you feel good**. Rather than break the habit, you want to keep on doing it. Over time, it becomes compulsive and you can no longer stop doing it even if you want to.

Rewiring the brain to overcome addiction

As you have seen, we can subconsciously use **neuroplasticity** to create an addiction or a "maladaptive behavior" in our mind. But neuroplasticity can also be the key to overcoming certain addictions.

Neuroscience has shown that in the case of addiction, *although certain neurons may have been permanently damaged*, the brain has the ability to heal itself – with your guidance – to shut down the damaged areas and **create new and healthy pathways. Yes this is all proven by scientific studies.**

The process is the same as we have previously discussed. We train the mind to replace the negative behavior with a positive one. Although individual neurons might be damaged beyond repair, it is still possible for the brain to create new pathways. **However, in the case of addiction, behavior has become compulsive and out of control, so additional tools are required. To follow are some of them.**

Mindfulness Meditation: Scientists and psychologists have discovered that meditation engages the mind, calms the body and raises self-awareness. It is so key to overcoming addiction that psychologists have developed what they call Mindfulness-Based Relapse Prevention or MBRP, which helps the brain create new responses to cravings and withdrawal distress.

Mindful meditation helps people with addictions control reactions to stress and discomfort, thus minimizing the chances of relapse. It also helps addicts develop healthy coping mechanisms like restfulness and inner peace.

The "Three Good Things Exercise" This technique is popular in the field of positive psychology and is commonly used to help addicts kick their habits. As you might have guessed, it involves recording in a journal three good things that happen in your life every day and how you are grateful for this. This exercise is also called "gratitude journaling". Neuroscience recognizes the amazing healing power of gratitude and how it reinforces the mind against negative thoughts and behaviors. The whole key is to transfer your focus from damaging negative thoughts to positive thoughts in the moment that anyone can conjure; due to the fact that almost everyone has something to be grateful for, like just being alive.

Creating Value Pathways. Values are the moral or religious beliefs that we embrace which can motivate us towards positive change. In cases of addiction especially, a strong value system can really help break addictive patterns and drive positive change.

Start with defining what your values are and repeating them out loud. These can be family values, such as, "My family is everything to me. I care too much about my children to harm them with my gambling..."

They can be religious values such as, "My faith prohibits heavy drinking. I need to repent and set things right with God..."

Work values can be important to you. "My porn addiction and late nights are detrimental to my success and advancement in my career..."

Values are in direct opposition to addiction and therefore, making them a part of your mind rewiring routine will achieve much faster results.

Create a "Recovery Loop". When you practice the above exercises regularly, the brain will start to learn that things like family, relationships, faith and work ethics give you more pleasure than your addiction. A recovery loop is then created and the adduction neural pathway gradually disappears, as it is no longer used.

Be honest with yourself

Recognizing that you have an addiction is the first step to recovery. This not a mere cliché but an absolute truth.

Neuroplasticity can be very successful in curing behavioral addictions and some substance addictions like smoking, prescription medication and caffeine addiction. But there are cases of extreme substance abuse such as addiction to heroin or long-term alcoholism, where medical and psychiatric intervention is necessary. So, be honest with yourself and if you need help, get it. Then you can incorporate neuroplasticity techniques from this chapter into your treatment.

Negative thinking addiction

Some people have an addiction to negative thinking. Negative thoughts can ruin someone's life without him or her even knowing why.

In this case, simple re-affirming positive thoughts slowly every hour daily can make tremendous improvements in a short period of time; such thoughts like **"every day in every way I am getting better and smarter"** will go a long way in ending the negative thought patterns. You can create as many positive affirmations as you want, just make sure they resonate with you.

Finally, don't give up! There may be setbacks along the way, but never lose hope that change is possible. It is and many have accomplished this.

Chapter 6: Affirmations

The first time I practiced affirmations I felt incredibly silly. They felt fake and awkward; even the sound of my voice repeating them was so forced and uncomfortable that I decided not to do them again. But I had done my research and knew that affirmations were another powerful tool for rewiring the mind and that the more tools I had in my toolbox, the better. So, I stuck to it. I stood in from of the mirror every morning, diligently repeating my affirmations and trying not to laugh. Over time, I realized they were indeed very powerful. Now, I do them effortlessly and with total conviction.

What are affirmations?

They are positive statements that you repeat to yourself which over time, will rewire your brain (neurons) to believe them.

Proponents of the Law of Attraction rely on affirmations to manifest or attract the things they want into their lives. They claim that by frequently and consistently throwing the statement out into the universe, its energy will attract and manifest it in your life. However, science has yet to provide conclusive evidence for this.

What science does tell us is that if you keep repeating something to your brain, it will learn to believe it and regulate your behavior according to that thought. Therefore, for our purpose, we use affirmations to rewire the mind.

The positive affirmations that we repeat to ourselves build self-belief in our subconscious mind. Some examples are:

- ***I trust myself to make the right choices every time.***

- ***I release my anger and am able to see clearly.***

- ***I follow my dreams no matter what.***

- ***Everything works out for my highest good.***

Some people make wild claims that affirmations will change your life but it's very unlikely that affirmations alone can do that. However, **affirmations can change your life for the better when used as part of the process to rewire the brain.**

How do Affirmations work?

1. Affirmations are statements that are not necessarily true but you repeat them with the conviction that they are true, thus "reprogramming" your subconscious mind to believe them.

2. They must always be stated in the present tense, and sometimes in the future tense in order to be effective.

3. They motivate you to overcome negative thoughts that are limiting you and holding you back from achieving what you want.

4. They inspire you to achieve goals and visualize future achievements.

5. They should be powerful statements that reflect what you want to become.

6. Repeating affirmations regularly reshapes inner beliefs about yourself and your perception of the world around you.

7. The goal is to change your outer world and the outcomes you achieve by first reshaping your inner beliefs.

8. As your mind creates these new positive beliefs, it becomes easier to shape your life into what you want it to be.

<u>**What science tells us about affirmations**</u>

There is increasing interest from the fields of neurology and psychology around how affirmations affect the brain. Research has already confirmed the following benefits:

- Studies have shown that optimistic people tend to live longer because they have healthier hearts. Daily affirmations increase your optimism, and therefore, may give you a healthier, longer lifespan.

- Affirmations enhance problem-solving skills, the ability to work under pressure and <u>cope with stressful situations</u>. This is especially helpful in situations of social anxiety and tight work deadlines.

- Affirmations enforce feelings of gratitude and flood your brain with good thoughts about all the blessings you have in your life. Your brain will then trigger feelings of happiness and optimism.

- Like meditation, affirmations make you more aware of your thoughts, so that you are more quickly able to challenge negative thoughts when they come up.

The right way to practice affirmations

Make a list of what you think are your negative qualities or behaviors. This could be anything from "I panic under pressure" or "I am a bad parent" or "I never see anything through", and so on. The list can also include what others see as negative qualities in you; criticisms your boss, friends or family have made because affirmations will help you challenge these.

Write down the affirmations that correspond to the above list. You can find thousands of them online and customize them for your own situation. Over time, you will learn how to write your own.

Affirmations must be positive. Never say, for example, "I am not a bad parent" or "I am not a failure". It's better to say "I am a good, caring parent" or "I succeed at anything I put my mind to"

Use the present tense. This is a no-brainer, since stating affirmations in the past tense is totally senseless. Some affirmations are also stated in the future tense, which is perfectly fine, such as "I will curb and control my craving for ice cream every time it comes up" or "I will not allow my smoking habit to control me".

State them with full conviction. This is the most difficult part and will require practice and repetition.

State them out loud. Affirmations must be spoken by you and read silently for them to be most effective. Voice the statement clearly and decisively, without rushing.

Schedule a time. There is no best or worse time to practice affirmations, although I would say that saying the first thing in the morning is a great way to start your day, as they will put you on a positive frame of mind and keep you inspired and upbeat. However, any other time during the day is perfectly fine. Some people prefer to say them directly before falling asleep.

Limit the number of affirmations you practice at any given time. Ideally, you should not practice more than 5 affirmations at one time for a certain length of time before moving on to new ones. Some people will use one affirmation that they practice for a whole month, while others will practice 3 or 4 for one or two weeks and so on. There is no right or wrong way other than your personal preference.

Repeat them as much as you can. If you can practice several times a day, great! It only takes about 5 minutes each time? Why is frequency important? Because the goal is to make your brain turn the affirmation into a truth. Therefore, frequent repetition over a certain timeframe is key.

<u>**Step by step practice exercise**</u>

1. Stand in from of the mirror and look yourself in the eye.

2. Take three very deep breaths, counting to 10 for each inhalation and exhalation.

3. State the affirmation clearly and really focus on the meaning of each word, letting it sink into your mind.

4. Repeat the affirmation 3 – 5 times.

5. End with another 3 deep breaths, visualizing that words you have just said are flowing through your body.

6. Note: if you are unable to do this in front of a mirror or don't feel comfortable, start the exercise from step 2.

Be patient!

Affirmations take time to work and really settle into your mind. Typically, it will be one month to several months before you begin to see their effects. So be patient and remember that rewiring the mind after years and years of negative thought processes just doesn't happen overnight – but the rewards are significant and totally worth the investment of your time and effort.

Types of affirmations

Affirmations can be used for almost any goals you can imagine; career, love, weight loss, health issues, fears and even affirmations for changing careers, a broken heart and the loss of a pet. Below is a good variety of affirmations that can be used in the process of rewiring the mind.

Affirmations for self-acceptance

We all have weak spots or faults that make us feel lacking, and these can be addressed with the following affirmations of self-acceptance.

- I have the power to change my world.

- I respect and love myself

- I accept myself just as I am

- I choose to focus on what I can control and trust that the rest will work out.

- I am proud of myself and what I have accomplished.

- I approve of myself completely and fully.

- Today, I choose me.

- I have everything I need within myself.

- I have much to celebrate about myself and my life.

- I choose to stop apologizing for being me.

- I say no with ease.

- I am growing and learning each and every day.

- Affirmations for mind healing

Many of us struggle with mental and emotional issues. The following affirmations will establish the belief that we can overcome them.

- My mind knows how to heal itself

- My mind is healing itself right now.

- Each day I am finding myself thinking more positively

- My mind is 100% focused on healing my body and mind

- I feel emotions without losing control

- I will deal with my emotions in a positive fashion

- Feelings are never right or wrong. They just are.

Affirmations for empowerment and mind motivation.

These affirmations are designed to motivate and empower you in all aspects of your life.

- I accept my power.

- I do have personal power.

- I am the author of my own destiny.

- I have all the power I need.

- Every experience I have is perfect for my growth.

- I am responsible for my own happiness.

- I am growing in wisdom, courage and good health,

- I get my work done effortlessly.

- I meet challenges bravely.

- I grow stronger each day.

Affirmations for mindfulness - We already know that mindfulness is vital to the rewiring of the mind. These powerful affirmations will help keep you grounded in the present.

- I now choose to live in the present.

- I enjoy being aware of the present moment.

- I can always handle the moment I'm in.

- All my power is in the present moment.

- There is no future... there is only the present.

- All that matters in this moment is what I am doing and how I am doing it.

- All that matters is how I spend this moment.

- Each moment contains clarity and truth that can revitalize my life.

- Every moment in my life is a new beginning.

- Every moment of my life is full of choices.

- I actively participate in the present NOW.

- The past is dead.

- I am perfect and whole in this moment

Affirmations for forgiveness - Dwelling on past grievances really cam harm us emotionally, especially when we find it hard to forgive people who have hurt us. The following affirmations will help to release those feelings and empower your mind, because there is strength in being able to forgive and release.

- I move beyond forgiveness to understanding and I have compassion and kindness for all.

- I am forgiving, loving, and compassionate.

- I am free from the prison of resentment.

- When I forgive myself, it becomes easier to forgive others.

- Forgiveness frees and releases me from that past.

- I am able to heal from the hurt of my past.

- I forgive so that I can have inner peace.

- I can only help others by forgiving myself.

- I forgive everyone in my past for all perceived wrongs.

Affirmations for gratitude - Gratitude is a great mind-healer and generator of positive thoughts. These affirmations will train your mind to focus on all of the blessings you have, rather than on the shortcomings of life.

- I am grateful for who I am and what I have.

- I am grateful to people who have brought positive energy into my life.

- I am grateful for every experience in my life.

- I count my blessings every day for them.

- I greet each day with joy and gratitude.

- I am thankful for simply being alive today

- I will be thankful for whatever life brings.

- I appreciate all, I give thanks, I am grateful.

- I am truly blessed.

Christian affirmations - For the more religiously inclined, these affirmations will give spiritual calm while enforcing your beliefs. For non-Christians, some of the words can be changed to suit your particular faith.

- God stands at my side and gives me the strength I need for today.

- I am able to be used by God.

- God reveals his spiritual truths to me by his Spirit.

- Christ has set me free.

- In God I find grace and mercy in time of need.

- God is my refuge, strength and help in times of trouble.

- Because I believe in Jesus, I no longer live in the darkness.

- I am created in the *image* of God.

- Affirmations for addiction - These addiction recovery affirmations will help you and give you the strength to fight your addiction.

- I am the only thing in control of my life.

- I deserve to be free of addiction.

- I forgive myself for what I did under the influence.

- My life is free of drugs.

- I can look inside myself as a source of joy.

- I am stronger than temptation.

- I am in control.

- I respect my body and my loved ones.

- Every day, in every way, I am getting better. (This is one of the most popular affirmations ever, created by Emile Coue: https://en.wikipedia.org/wiki/%C3%89mile_Cou%C3%A9).

To conclude, affirmations are a perfect addition to your mind rewiring routine and are beneficial for your mind and body. When practiced with meditation, the can be a powerful tool indeed.

Chapter 7: Evaluate the Company You Keep

Friendship, romantic relationship, and family ties impact us far more than we may like to allow. Your friends may be building you up or holding you back. Your parents may have the best intention but may not be able to support your development or growth. Even your spouse may have shortcomings when it comes to mental support.

Mental support is the issue that we'll tackle here. Now you should by no means run out for a divorce order simply because your spouse doesn't understand your mental development needs.

You should; however, consider making a few new friends, the internet has made that more accessible than ever before. Psychological support is vital for reaching goals of mental improvement or self-betterment.

Why is mental support so important? Your brain handles stressors with more considerable bravery and a calm composure when friends, family, or even acquaintances are nearby. This result could be because you're trying to lessen the appearance of a threat or to divert your own attention. The Association for Psychological Science offered a statement that gives a lot of insight into the effect of the company, "Alone, the world is a lot more demanding."

Aside from the mental stimulus response to the presence of friends, we have less analytical support. The people around you shape who you are currently. Yes, you likely have static aspects of your personality, such as your sense of humor, or lifelong preferences. If you doubt the impact that the people around you can have, consider the following statements. As you read through them acknowledge if you believe them to be true, or false.

If no one in your life participates in a particular hobby you enjoy, you are less likely to pursue that hobby.
Friend groups will often have two or more shared activities or preferences.
People around you will exchange information regularly.

Spending time with people socially can allow you to construct new perspectives.
If you believed that any of these were true, then you have already bought into the concept that the people around you can shape the way you think. Scientists worked with a group of approximately 47 college students and found that "friends" who spent time together outside of class responded similarly to videos.

The videos used in this study varied from an actor practicing improv to a wedding between two men, and a short film about the risks of sports in college. The thing is that the concept of homophily, or the idea that we prefer to make friends who visually look similar to ourselves, transcended outer appearance. During this study, it showed that friends, whether they visually resembled each other or not had similar brain activity.

When friends saw the same videos, the mental imaging taken at the time was eerily similar.

 They thought the same jokes were funny, and the corresponding risks assessed provoked the same level of threat response. The similarity in these responses was so significant and consistent they could use elimination variables including religion, economic level, and even ethnic group. Essentially this study proved that your friends think the same and respond the same to information.

It would be easy to say, "That's not true; my friend and I have different political views." That difference of opinion may be present in the filtered and carefully thought out the response you have when discussing politics. On a simple action and response level, you and your friend likely have more similar views than you might have imagined possible.

Jim Rohn famously captured this concept in a quote, **"We are the average of the five people we spend the most time with."** This quote relies on the law of averages, which works on the notion that anything will be the average of all possible outcomes.

Are you comfortable seeing and responding to your environment the same way your friends do? These are people you love and have probably spent years with, does that mean the price of friendship is your development? No, but carefully consider the restrictions that your association places on you.

Can you push your friends to expand their horizons and participate in learning or experiencing something new with you? Yes, but that's not necessarily your job. As part of your brain training, you may realize the mental models that the people around you put to work and which ones they avoid. Additionally, you might see how they can easily accept some things that they know as truths, a semantic memory, while you begin to question them.

The most significant solution to the problem that comes with friendships impact on your brain abilities is to make more friends. You don't have to give up your current friends and giving up your family is not an available option for many people. However, when you make new friends, you can somewhat shop around for what you're looking for in your life.

Making new friends affects that law of averages mentioned with the Jim Rohn quote. By adding more factors into your life, you can offset some limiting beliefs of the people around you. More than anything else, though, our brains perform best when we are making new relationships. Friendships more than family ties or romantic relationships show the larges boost in the reward center of the brain, the basal ganglia. You might recall that this is the same region of the brain where we store many implicit memories and form new habits. As you start to piece together how your mind processes aspects of interaction, it's easy to see the bigger picture.

When making new friends, you are creating new memories. New friends, in particular, spark a more excellent feeling of reward as these are more implicit memories of social interaction. You're identifying and analyzing this new person, recording their preferences and reactions to your statements. As you build more memories, your brain shifts, creating episodic memories with that person where the focus becomes on the moment rather than the minute actions between two people.

Making friends is good for you, and it's clear that your brain benefits from it. Additionally, our brain will grow a little stagnant when spending too much time with the same people. You'll adopt more limiting beliefs and narrower ranges of perception than if you were spending more time with different people referencing back to the law of averages.

So how can making new friends play a fun role in brain training?

Well, there are a few different ways to implement this aspect of building up your brainpower by making new friends or increasing positive friend time:

- Set a quota for new people to meet each week or month.

- Schedule time to see people that you want to spend more time with regularly.

- Join an online community and interact with others.

- Change the way you interact with your current relationships.

- Host a potluck for coworkers, current friends, or extended family you don't see often. Host some sort of fun event.

- Encourage friends to bring their friends to an event you signed up for.

- Sign up with Meetup.com to meet real people near you that have similar interests.

- Join or create a club in your loca area for specific interests or hobbies, or create your own Meetup group.

- Take a class at community college, or a onetime event class.

- Start saying, "Yes" to invitations that you would usually turn down.

Diving into some of these tips a little more will help you decide which ones you are comfortable with and how much you want to change your social network.

To start making new friends, set a monthly or weekly quota. Many people actively avoid introducing themselves or engaging with another adult. A childhood skill that dies soon into high school has two primary purposes. First, people avoid forging new relationships because they fear being vulnerable. Second, people avoid meeting someone new because they don't know what those cards hold. In a society that has much more extensive access to news now than ever before, people have become scary.

Strangers are the enemy.

Ever move into a new neighborhood and you got the cold shoulder from most of the neighbors? That's because you are an unknown to them.

While it might seem like that lady walking her dog at the park you run past could be a serial killer, she's probably not. Remember the mental model of Hanlon's Razor, the attribution of malice is least likely. At that rate, you can employ Occam's Razor as well. It is improbable that the person you want to introduce yourself to will approach you with any form of malice.

There is no question, though. When you first start introducing yourself to people, you will get a few weird looks. Not only are people not accustomed to someone walking up to them in public anymore, but also they may have the same fears of exposed vulnerability.

They may even think that you're out to cause them harm. As you introduce yourself to more and more people, you'll see that your initial confidence will impact the response you receive.

Example script in meeting new people:

"Hi, I'm (name), and I (run/walk/eat) here all the time. I (like/see) your (object which grabbed your attention) and was interested. I wanted to say hi."

In a real-world context, this might be:

"Hi, I'm John, and I eat here all the time. I saw your book and was interested. I wanted to say hi." Then you would utilize that object which caught your attention to begin a conversation. In this example, you can say that you have not read it yet, or that reading is a hobby you enjoy.

Alternatively, you can find an online community for nearly anything. From online book clubs, makeup communities, auto sports forums, and even Dungeons and Dragons-style roleplaying games.

The internet has made it easier than ever to make new friends. Additionally, there is no surface-level fear of having to prompt interaction. When joining an online community, you will have a built-in opportunity for initiating communication. A simple, hey what was last week's book? Or "I'm new to playing D&D can someone help?"

Online communities can, indeed be harsh. There are many people out there who work their way into these communities with the intent of getting out their frustrations or causing discord. However, each community should have moderators and administrators to respond and divert these users.

The most important aspect of being part of an online community is to participate. Remember that your brain responds to interactions, not commentary. If you're lurking, or just reading through threads and not responding, then you're not getting any of the benefits that come with making new friends.

If you're having trouble, resort to a fun and modern-day solution, use Meetup. Meetup is an online service where you can find groups that meet physically in your area. To start, you select a subject that interests you, then find a group that meets a convenient time and location. The great thing about using Meetup access a new social circle is that everything is already built-in and controlled through a third party.

You have a commonality or subject that everyone can discuss, you meet somewhere that is convenient for everyone, and everyone there goes with the intent of meeting new people.

A common but useful brain training tip is to start saying, "Yes." It's become a joke that people say no to invitations because they would rather stay home and binge-watch a show. The thing is, your brain is sorely missing out on a lot of mental exercises. When you go out to an event, dinner, or anything similar, you're practicing all of your socialization skills at once.

Generally speaking, if someone has thought of you enough to invite you to something personally, say yes. For more open invitations such as a Facebook event, do something with a friend that you don't see so often. Play the rule of averages to your benefit. You might find that this person has a hobby that falls in line with one of your brain training games. There are opportunities everywhere, if only you say yes.

Remember that when founding new friendships, you are both getting something out of the interaction. Science suggests that people with stronger social connections were even less likely to die. Those who have weakened ties or are outright lonely will experience the same risk factors of smoking 15 or more cigarettes per day, being an alcoholic, or being overweight.

Another part of the social health focus is that when you focus on the group, you take on responsibility for these other people. In turn, you must take better care of yourself to set an example and continue fulfilling your responsibility to them. But how can you be sure that you're going to meet the "right" people or people that you want to be around and to grow with?

It's easy. Use your values and your interests to forge your new friendships. For example, if you're looking for someone also interested in brain training, look for someone who enjoys reading or math games. If you see someone buying a Sudoku puzzle book, introduce yourself. Alternatively, someone who listens to self-help podcasts might be someone who is open to exploring new perspectives rather than employing limited ones.

As an adult making new friends is a challenge. Friendships and other social ties significantly impact your mental health and wellbeing. As part of your brain training program, you should set a quota on meeting new people regularly, whether it is online or in person. Use these new friendships to put your different mental models to work and expand your perception of the world around you.

Chapter 8: Techniques to Improve Your Memory

Memory lapses may be caused by distractions, preoccupation, lack of focus and weakened memory muscle. There are numerous techniques to beef up your brain muscles:

Give your brain a workout.

By the time you are an adult, your brain has already formed millions of neural pathways necessary in processing and recalling information quickly, solving easily recognizable problems, and executing common tasks almost instantaneously. But sticking to these timeworn pathways, you are denying your brain the stimulation it needs to keep growing and developing. Your brain needs some shaking up from time to time!

The "use it or lose it" principle popular in building muscular strength also applies to memory enhancement. The more you subject your brain to intellectual activities, the better you'll be at remembering information. The best brain exercises take you out of your routine and challenge you to form new brain pathways.

Good brain-boosting activities have the following elements:

- **It introduces you to something new.** An activity may be considered intellectually demanding, but if it is something that you've already mastered, then it doesn't qualify as a good brain exercise. The activity needs to be something that you haven't yet tried and is out of your comfort zone. It's your exposure to learning new things and developing new skills that eventually strengthen your brain.

- **It's difficult and challenging.** The best brain-boosting activities should be hard enough to demand your full attention. But as soon as you've mastered the activity, it won't require as much mental effort anymore and won't challenge you as much as when you were introduced to it for the first time. For example, learning to play a challenging new piece of music on the piano counts. Playing a tough piece you've already memorized does not.

- **It's a skill you can improve on.** Search out activities that let you begin at an easy level and move up as your expertise progresses and your capabilities improve. When a once difficult level starts to feel comfortable, that means it's time to move on to the next level of difficulty.

- **It's fulfilling.** A sense of fulfillment encourages the brain's learning process. It keeps you engaged and interested. As a result, you are more likely to continue doing it and the greater the rewards you'll reap. So choose activities that, while challenging, are still enjoyable and satisfying.

Think of an activity you've always wanted to try—learning how to play a musical instrument, speaking a foreign language, playing chess, or making pottery. So long as an endeavor keeps you engaged, they are sure to help you improve your memory.

<u>Engage in physical exercise.</u>

Mental exercise is important for brain health especially when coupled with physical exercise. Physical activities help your brain stay sharp by increasing oxygen supply to your brain and reducing the risks for disorders that affect memory retention such as diabetes and cardiovascular diseases. Exercise also encourages secretion of helpful hormones that put stress and depression in check. Perhaps the most important benefit exercise has on the brain is in neuroplasticity, by stimulating new neuronal pathways known to improve memory formation and recall.

Physical Exercises that are Good for the Brain

- Aerobic Exercises

In most cases, aerobic exercises that are good for your heart are good for your brain as well.

Here's how cardio exercises benefit your brain:

- Aerobic exercises repair damaged brain cells thereby improving brain function.

- Cardio exercises encourage secretion of the happy hormone dopamine. This makes you feel relaxed and happier. Regular exercise in general alleviates symptoms of depression in people.

- Aim for 120 minutes of moderate cardio exercise each week. You may dedicate an hour swimming in the morning and another hour in the evening for dancing.

- Stick to your exercise plan. Make it a habit and a part of your daily regular routine. It would help if you do it with an exercise buddy, so you could encourage each other.

- Don't push yourself to your limits. An intense exercise wouldn't do more good in decreasing your anxiety levels than an exercise done in moderation. If you are just starting, 30 minutes of moderate exercise will already do you wonders.

- Yoga

Yoga, when coupled with meditation, helps focus and calm your mind. Needless to say, it reduces stress and keeps the brain in tiptop shape.

- It's also known to extend your life by slowing down cellular aging.

- People who regularly meditate often say that they feel more positive, and that a happy disposition enables them to deal better with daily life challenges.

- Walking

While walking is the simplest and probably the least costly exercise you can do, it is known to greatly improve brain performance.

- Regular walks enable different parts of your brain to communicate with each other. It has something to do with the neural pathways that are strengthened during regular walks. This enhancement of the neural connections makes you better at planning, strategizing, prioritizing, and multi-tasking.

- Also, practically everyone can enjoy a good walk, regardless of their level of fitness or age.

- Jogging or Running

If you are a person with a lot of energy that needs burning, jogging or running are the best forms of exercise you can do at the start of the day.

- A 15-minute run will help reduce that extra energy to a level you need to get through your work for the rest of the day without getting distracted.

- A quick run will also help you bring on a rush of the mood-booster hormone serotonin.

- Group Classes

For motivation and inspiration, consider joining group classes. You'd always look forward to working out because exercising becomes play more than a boring activity. Plus there's nothing more rewarding than making new friends.

For group activities, you may consider Aqua Zumba, Latin Hip-hop, Family Yoga, Tai Chi, or Group Cycling.

Chew gum while learning new things.

Studies correlate chewing gum with increased heart rate levels resulting to increased circulation of oxygen-bearing blood into the brain. This in turn increases activity in the hippocampus, that part of the brain mainly responsible for forming memories.

Move your eyes sideways.

Make this a part of your daily morning exercise. Move your eyes from side to side for 30 seconds. Why? In studies, it was found out that horizontal eye movements strengthen the corpus callosum, a bundle of neuronal fibers that link the brain hemispheres: the creative right brain and the logical left brain.

Clench your fists.

There was a study conducted to determine how body parts may be linked to how the brain functions. It showed that clenching the hands improves a person's ability to memorize things. Making a fist with the right hand aided in learning something, and switching to making a fist with the left helped in recall.

At first, it seems farfetched that a person's hands have something to do with memory. The explanation given was that the hand-clenching stimulates the brain in a cross-wired manner. Making a fist with your right hand activates the left side of your brain; and the reverse happens with clenching the left hand.

Use unusual fonts.

Funky fonts promote better recall. There actually was a study that backs up this observation. So if you wonder how making something hard to read makes it easier to remember, here's the explanation: Think of the time you've skimmed through text, got to the end, and then realized that you didn't quite understand what the document said. The study explained that unusual fonts act like speed bumps.

Changing the font to make it harder to read will slow you down so you'd read more carefully, consequently improving your recall. A more complex explanation has something to do with confidence.

When you encounter a writing that's hard to decipher, you become less confident of your ability for comprehension. As you feel nervous about not understanding the material, you concentrate harder and go through it more deeply.

Doodle.

There's nothing like a blank sheet of paper to entice the brain to doodle. Research shows that doodling helps you let loose your imagination. Moreover, creating illegible drawings and writing down random thoughts encourages the brain to improve creative thinking, to stay focused and to retain information.

<u>**Laugh.**</u>

Laughter helps lower levels of cortisol, the hormone associated with stress. When secreted in high levels, cortisol is known to affect the hippocampus, the short-term memory consolidator, consequently impairing learning and memory.

Humor should be incorporated in your total wellness plan for excellent quality of life full of memories.

Start with these basics if you are looking for ways to bring more laughter in your life:

- **Take yourself less seriously.** Share your embarrassing moments and learn to laugh at yourself.

- **When you hear laughter, gravitate toward it.** You notice that you are always happy to share something funny because sharing feeds off the humor and affords you the chance to laugh again. So if you hear laughter, you knew that you just have to seek it out and join in.

- **Spend time with playful, fun people.** There are people who laugh heartily at themselves and at the absurdities of life. They are quick to find the humor in everyday situations. Their positive point of view and happy disposition are just contagious.

- **Surround yourself with images that lighten you up.** Put up a humorous poster in your office. Set a computer screensaver that never fails to make you smile. Display photos of you and your loved ones having fun.

- **Learn from children.** Pay attention to children and realize that they are the experts on playing, laughing, and taking life lightly.

Practice good posture.

Posture is often neglected as a conscious expression of one's self. You may not be doing it right, good news is it's possible to make improvements on how you hold yourself, how it can ideally shape your life and future accomplishments.

In a series of experiments, it was discovered that body posture can affect the recall of both positive and negative memories. When sitting in a slouch and looking downward, study participants found it much easier to recall helpless and negative memories than empowering and positive ones. When sitting upright with chins up, it's always easy for participants to remember optimistic memories.

A straight posture generally improves memory because sitting upright encourages increased blood flow and oxygen to the brain by as much as 40 percent.

Feast on a Mediterranean diet.

Researches show that a diet of fruits, vegetables, nuts, and fish (a whole range of food that is common in most Mediterranean fares) is not only good for your heart but for your brain as well. Vegetables and nuts are likely to fend off memory loss especially in late adulthood. Fruits and Omega-3 in fish are anti-oxidants that will protect you from cognitive decline.

Take caffeine-rich drinks to enhance your memory consolidation.

Whether it's a cup of tea, a can of soda, or a mug of freshly brewed coffee, consumption of caffeine is the chosen energy booster for people who want to wake up or stay up. Studies have found another use for this stimulant; a memory enhancer.

Although most of these studies found that caffeine has little effect in creating new memories, the substance has actually improved memory recall. Research has identified caffeine to be a major player in memory consolidation, a process where memories created were strengthened leading to deeper level of memory retention and that therefore the substance is better ingested after learning a task.

Be careful, though, to check if caffeine seems to interfere with your sleep at night. If it does, reduce intake or cut it off altogether.

Meditate to improve your working memory.

The working memory could be likened to a chalkboard, where you temporarily "write" bits of information like the location details of a place you are visiting for the first time or names and faces of people you meet in an event. You hang on to these chunks of data until you are ready to sort them into those that you let go entirely (because you have no use for them anymore) or those that you commit to long-term memory (for later recall and use).

Working memory is the same place where you do quick mental computations and hold random details when engaged in conversation.

How does meditation help strengthen the working memory? Studies show that regular meditation enhances your ability to focus. Meditation will enable you to have more control over your alpha rhythm, when your brain experiences small smooth bursts of electricity sending you into a state of complete relaxation. This not only improves your creativity but it enables you to filter out all distractions making it easy for you to store important things to memory.

Have a good night's sleep.

Sleep is an important factor in memory storage. It is during slow-wave sleep that the hippocampus replays all the events that happened during your waking moments. Working under compressed time, it sorts through your experiences as it files away those which are relevant while discarding those that won't be significant in the future.

Cultivate a good sleeping habit by doing the following:

- Commit to a regular sleep schedule by going to bed at the same time every night and getting up at the same time every morning. Don't break your routine, even on weekends and holidays.

- Avoid TVs, phones, computers, and tablets an hour before bed. The blue light emitted by these gadgets triggers wakefulness by suppressing secretion of melatonin that induces sleepiness.

If you suspect that caffeine keeps you up at bedtime, reduce your intake or cut it out entirely. There are people who are overly sensitive to caffeine that even coffee taken in the morning interferes with sleep at night.

Pay attention.

Do you remember that time when you were planning to buy a red Chevrolet and suddenly you noticed that what catches your attention during your daily commute are all the red cars plying your route. Pieces of information are committed to your memory because you are interested in them. When you develop a fascination for things around you, you automatically observe important details and get them laser-etched on your brain.

Make time for friends.

We are social animals not meant to survive in isolation. Relationships stimulate our brains. As a matter of fact, connecting with others may very well be the best kind of brain exercise.

Research shows that maintaining worthwhile friendships and a support system are vital not only to mental and emotional health, but to brain health as well. In a study conducted by the Harvard School of Public Health, researchers discovered that individuals with active social lives had the slowest rate of memory decline.

There are ways you could take advantage of the memory-boosting benefits of socializing, such as volunteering, joining a club, or reaching out to someone over the phone.

Concentrate.

There are no fast-charging shortcuts to increasing your concentration. Today's world is so full of distractions; not to mention the huge volume of information that we need to process every day. We simply just cannot sort through all the information we are bombarded with day in and day out.

Then there's the challenge of determining what information to keep and how to recall them fast. The secret here is to tackle big issues first so your brain won't be pre-occupied with matters that may unnecessarily clutter available brain storage space.

Use Mnemonics.

Another effective tool in memorization is called mnemonics. A mnemonics is a tool (a rhyme, an acronym, an image, or a phrase) to help you remember facts or large amounts of information.

There are different types of mnemonic devices, namely:

Visual image. The trick is to associate a word or a name with a visual image that is colorful, vivid, and three-dimensional. Example: To remember the name Robert Goldman, who works as an inspirational speaker, you may conjure an image that you can associate with him, like a golden robot (which sounds like Robert) that is talking non-stop (his work involves speaking.)

Acrostic. Create a sentence where the first letter of each word represents the initial of what it is you want to remember. Example: "My Very Excited Mother Just Served Us Nine Pies" where the first letter of each word is the first letter of the planets in our Solar System in order (Mercury, Venus, Earth, Mars, Jupiter, Saturn, Uranus, Neptune, and Pluto); or if without Pluto: "My Very Educated Mother Just Served Us Noodles."

Acronym. An acronym is a word formed to represent the first letters of all the words that make up a group of keywords or ideas. Example: The acronym "HOMES" will help you recall the names of the Great Lakes: Huron, Ontario, Michigan, Erie, and Superior.

Rhymes. Rhymes are effective ways to remember more common facts and figures. Example: To remember which months have 30 days and which ones have 31, the following rhyme is helpful: "30 days hath September, April, June, and November. 28 days makes February fine, but in a leap year it has 29.

Chunking. Chunking is breaking up a series of characters or a long list of numbers into more manageable, easy to remember portions. Example: Breaking a 10-digit number (say 5558765903) into three sets of numbers (555-876-5903) makes memorizing it a lot easier.

Method of loci. Also known as the memory palace, memory journey, or mind palace technique, this mnemonic device works by imagining placing items you want to remember along a familiar route or specific places in a familiar building (or "palace") or room. Example: For a shopping list, picture a puddle of milk in the entryway to your house, eggs sitting on the sofa, slices of bread scattered up the stairs, and bananas on your bed.

Sing.

Music is not only an excellent mood enhancer but a good memory tool as well. Singing exercises the right side of the brain. Consequently, it makes you perform better at problem solving. Ever notice how you can easily rhyme words when you are singing them than when you are speaking them? This is because the song's melody has activated the pattern recognition ability of the right side of your brain.

Stay Curious.

Always have good appetite for learning new things and an unquenchable thirst for new knowledge. This is one of the most effective pieces of advice you can get to keep your brain in tiptop shape. Learning a new concept every now and then heightens your awareness. Consequently, heightened awareness leads to understanding. It goes without saying that everything you understood, you'd easily remember. For example, knowing that the value of pi is the ratio between the circumference of a circle and its diameter, you are sure that it is a constant value because no matter the size of the circle, it is always the same shape. Interestingly, the value of pi is an irrational number that goes on and on. But you can memorize the first 7 digits of pi by remembering this sentence: "How I wish I could calculate pi." Count the number of letters in each word. It will give you 3.141592.

Read.

We can also gauge the memory power of a person by the size of his vocabulary. Effective speakers will tell you that they do it by reading as much as they can devour. If you don't have the luxury of time, you may build your vocabulary by learning one word each day. To reinforce commitment to memory, use your word-of-the-day at every opportunity by using it in your interactions. That is easily 365 words a year, more than enough words to make a good impression during conversations.

Chapter 9: The Pitfalls of Overthinking

The process of rewiring your mind requires that you avoid negative influences, to keep your mind fresh and relaxed for optimal rewiring results. One of the biggest negative influences that can obstruct your progress is overthinking.

Overthinking is different from thinking things through. There are certain decisions or actions that need to be thought through very carefully – in fact, not thinking them through could have hazardous outcomes. For example, say your company offers you the position of heading a new regional office, which would require you and your family to relocate overseas for three years. That is the kind of decision that requires hours if not days of pondering and this is perfectly healthy and desirable.

But spending 10 minutes trying to decide what to have for breakfast, which tie to wear, or spending hours comparing goods before making a purchase is, in the larger scheme of things, pretty trivial and a waste of time.

Overthinking also includes running past conversations or encounters in our heads over and over again, and *looking for hidden signs or meanings,* or thinking that we should have said this rather than that. It also includes envisioning future scenarios, all the things that could go wrong, what you should say in case of this or that... in short, overloading your mind with useless thoughts that have no ;logical basis. You can't go back and redo what has happened, nor will worrying or overanalyzing give you the ability to control what happens in the future.

Keep in mind this simple equation: Overthinking leads to worry. Worry leads to stress. Stress causes stress response and panic attacks. Moreover, overthinking can lead **to crippling uncertainty, where you are unable to decide on even the simplest thing, and you lose control over your life**.

Overthinking leads to two types of destructive thought patterns:

- Ruminating

- Worrying.

<u>Ruminating involves rehashing things over and over again, thinking,</u>

"I shouldn't have said that; that made me look really bad..."

"Maybe If I'd dressed more conservatively I'd have gotten the job".

"I should have done this instead. Now I've blown my chances..."

"I wasn't clear enough. He/ she probably misunderstood what I meant..."

"That email wasn't phrased well. I should have mentioned..."

No further explanation is needed here.

It's pretty clear that this thought pattern is extremely detrimental to anyone who gets caught up in it. In addition, it's usually not accompanied by positive self-talk like, "We all make mistakes, I'll make sure not to do that again in a similar situation".

Worrying is a form of overthinking where your mind leaps ahead and imagines failures or disastrous outcomes to things that haven't happened yet, such as:

"I haven't studied well enough. What if I fail the exam? I won't be able to graduate this year..."

"The weather's bad and it's getting dark. I'm worried my spouse will have an accident driving home..."

"My doctor says the surgery is simple and safe but what if I have complications? What if they get worse and I die? "

Worrying and ruminating are two thought patterns bombard your brain with a constant stream of unhealthy and unproductive thoughts. If left unchecked, you will be dragged into a vicious cycle that will eat away at your very sanity.

Some pitfalls of overthinking

- Impairs judgment because it keeps your brain in constant fog of fear and indecision.

- Elevates stress levels

- Creates chronic indecision which can totally destroy self-confidence over time, and cause depression

- Burns up mental and physical energy to the point where you can either get physically sick or develop a ***mental disorder***

- Leads you to mistrust feeling happy

Stress Response and panic attacks are a direct outcome of overthinking

The stress response is also known as the "fight or flight" response. It is vital for our safety in times of real danger, such as a shooting, God forbid, or some other violent situation. The stress response releases certain hormones in our body (including the well-known adrenalin rush) that trigger a heightened pulse and heart rate, dilated pupils, shaking and intense fear and alertness. Having a stress response when there is no real danger can really wreak havoc on your mind and body.

A panic attack triggers the same response when constant anxiety builds up.

A stress response or panic attack is followed by what is called the "relaxation response", when your body calms down and its functions return to normal. This commonly takes between 20 to 30 minutes. Every time you have a stress response or panic attack, you are pushing your mind and body to extremes that over time, will take their toll on your health. It's no surprise that stress is the number one cause of high blood pressure, stroke, heart disease, diabetes and many other serious illnesses. This alone should a huge motivator for rewiring the brain.

12 Tips for Rewiring your mind to stop overthinking

Overthinking is a habit and as we have learned, habits are hard to break because you have to train your mind to abandon the old neural pathways and create new ones. Again, constant practice is the key here.

Use the following tips help rewire your mind for overthinking:

Catch yourself doing it. Be on the lookout! When you find yourself overthinking, stop immediately. Go and do something else that will divert your focus; solve a crossword puzzle, meditate, do yoga, or read a few pages of a book. Choose an activity that will allow your brain to stay focused on the task at hand and not start to wander again to that phone call you had last week or the meeting with your boss next week.

Schedule time for thinking and decision-making. Write down any problems you need to solve or decisions you need to make. Schedule a specific time to sit down and think calmly and reasonably. Stay alert. If you catch yourself overthinking, stop yourself immediately.

Set deadlines for making decisions and stick to them. Depending on the issue, you can allot yourself 10 minutes, half an hour or an hour. Be firm with yourself and stick to the deadline.

For example, you've been asked to coordinate a bake sale for your local church. Realistically, you would need no more than 5 minutes to review your schedule, decide if you would enjoy doing it, and reply with a yes or no. On the other hand, if your boss offers you a promotion which would mean more money but longer working hours, you may need more to weigh all the options and decide if it worth it. You may even need to sleep on and see if you still feel the same way the next day.

Practice mindfulness. We will discuss mindfulness skills in another chapter because they are crucial tools to keep your mind focused on the present, rather than overthinking abbot the past or the future

Accept that you are doing your best. Affirm to yourself that you have always done your best in past situations and will do your best in the future. Tell yourself that yes, you have made mistakes but on the whole, you always manage to do pretty well.

Don't expect perfection. Perfection in anything is very rare, so it's unreasonable to expect things to go exactly the way we want. It's good to be ambitious and strive for the best but not to fret or worry over outcomes that are less than perfect.

Don't personalize. Not everything that happens in your life is necessarily about you. If your boss returns your "good morning" with a grumpy "Hi", don't run to your office and start pulling your hair out thinking he's planning to fire you Maybe he has family issues or is going through a personal crisis that has nothing to do with you at all. The clerk at the store who is a little short with you may not be feeling well. Taking everything personally leads to feelings of victimhood, which are very unhealthy. It also makes you insensitive to other people's feeling and circumstance so that you appear selfish and unkind. This is why empath is an important quality to develop through meditation, as we will see later.

Challenge your fears. Just because something didn't work out in the past doesn't mean you're doomed to failure forever. Every new beginning is a new chance to succeed and to shine. Confront and challenge your fears using the neuroplasticity process discussed earlier: acknowledge, confront, challenge and change. Train your brain to see every new beginning as an opportunity, a new adventure that you are excited about and eager to experience.

Think of what can go right. Overthinking is triggered by fear. If you do need to think something out and find yourself going off on a negative tangent, rewire your mind by challenging the thought and then thinking of all the things that could go right. Visualize yourself in that situation and how you would feel. Start to create a new and positive neural pathway.

Put things into perspective. Shut down overthinking by asking yourself how much a particular issue will really matter in two years, six months, a month, and so on. Changing time frames puts the issue into perspective and helps you realize that its overall impact on your life will not be devastating. Tis will shift your outlook and make you feel more positive

Get enough sleep. A good night's sleep is the best "brain balancer" there is. A well-rested mind and body is the magic charm that helps us think calmly, weight options realistically and see things in perspective. A jittery and sleep-starved brain is more prone to overthinking, anxiety and worry.

Be grateful. Each night before you go to bed, make a mental list of all the positive things that have happened throughout the day and the things and people you are grateful for. Stop yourself if you start dwelling on the negative and think pf someone you love, your partner or your child, and how grateful you are to have them in your life. Be grateful that they are happy and healthy and that they give you so much joy. You will find that next to that, anything else really is pretty insignificant. This exercise will help you drift off to sleep with nothing but positive, loving thoughts in your head.

What science tells us about overthinking

Overthinking is a result of growing older and becoming more cynical and disillusioned about life. Scientists have found that when we lose our childhood curiosity and wonder, we become more prone to worrying and overthinking. To a child, everything is wondrous and new; life is a great adventure waiting to be explored and each new discovery is more wonderful than the last. A child's brain makes billions of positive connections when that child is at the peak of curiosity.

We can regain some of those childhood qualities by observing children at play, playing with our own children or grandchildren and relearning to see the world through their eyes. What a fun and easy way to rewire our brain with optimism and joy!

Conclusion

So, what can we take away from all of this?

Quite simply, our brain is the most valuable asset we have, it's in your best interest to protect and build it. It is the control center of our body, the awesome computer that dictates and regulates our every action, thought and emotion. But when a computer gets overloaded with old files and folders, outdated programs and other useless and obsolete crap, it starts to slow down and experience glitches and bugs. Our brain is exactly the same. If it gets overburdened with negative thoughts and emotions, it causes glitches and freezes in your life flow.

If we don't make the decision to declutter, debug and reprogram our brain, it can become our biggest enemy. If will hold you back from experiencing life, from taking that step forward because you're too worried about failing. Your bad memories, subconscious beliefs and negative perceptions are just like those obsolete, outdated programs on a computer.

You can install new functional programs, overwrite those old files and bring your brain back to life... you need to rewire your brain actually...do it.

Helpful Links and Research Sources:

1. *Neuroplasticity published reports:*

    a. https://www.ncbi.nlm.nih.gov/pmc/articles/PMC4026979/